the flap pamp~

Where We're Going, We Don't Need Roads

open, read, turn

Where We're Going, We Don't Need Roads
the flap pamphlet series (No. 13)
Printed and Bound in the United Kingdom

Published by the flap series, 2015
the pamphlet series of flipped eye publishing

Cover Design by Petraski
Series Design © flipped eye publishing, 2010

Acknowledgements to the editors and staff of the following for
publishing versions of poems that appear in this pamphlet:
Poetry Review (The Ends of the Earth), **Popshot** (You Can Be Your Own
Mother**), Poems in Which** (Poem in Which Aliens Invade my Bedroom)
and **Rhyming Thunder: The Alternative Book of Young Poets** (1.21
Gigawatts & Percussion)

ISBN-13: 978-1-905233-47-2
Editorial work for this series is supported by the Arts Council of England

LOTTERY FUNDED

for Leanna and my family

Where We're Going,
We Don't Need Roads

"As long as you hit that wire with the connecting hook at precisely eighty-eight miles per hour, the instant the lightning strikes the tower… everything will be fine." – Dr Emmett Brown

Amy Acre

"Amy Acre writes with undeleted internet history, spilt whiskey on the tabletop and lipstick on collars. The doubts you have about everyone you kiss: they're an Amy Acre poem." – Tim Wells

"Amy Acre is one of the best new poets around - her poems are full of grit and love, looking at the world from fresh new angles. A vital presence on the poetry scene." – John Osborne

"While Amy Acre was performing, a bottle of champagne spontaneously erupted. I'm not even exaggerating, that happened." – Sabotage Reviews

Contents |

Where We're Going, We Don't Need Roads

Table for One at Wagamama

You reek of nothing.

Your voice, dead air like the sound waiters hear
when someone orders tap water.

Look at you, trying to be a person

with your steam punk crowd sourced polysexuality
with your actionable blue sky left wing agnosticism
and your flawless apostrophe usage.

Go and write a book
go and build a toilet in Malawi
go and pop midget replicas from your vagina
until your being hums white-hot with the freshly-baked heaven
of your superior knowledge
and your life is flung open like a window.

Look at you, trying to write a poem.

Don't you know meta's over?
It died the moment your finger hit the keys
the way Jeremy Clarkson killed jeans.

1.21 Gigawatts

Steal plutonium from Libyan terrorists.
Leave them a shoddy bomb casing
stuffed with the guts of an old pinball machine.

Take me to your bed sweats and dead end stories
that get lost and end up in Morden.

Take me back to the future we'll never have.

Give me ornamental sheep and waterlogged teeth
so our kisses
echo.

Set the time circuits twenty years from now
and show me how you midlife crisis.
We'll ride through your fat Elvis years,
your alarming flirtation with crystal healing.

Send cables streaming in a bruise of sky.
Wrap fingers tight round a bolt of lightning.

Show me worthless fights
and you missing my fortieth birthday
to drive Tony to the airport.

Abort the embryos of memories.
Let our thirty-something stalemates wrinkle backwards.
Shed them to powder.

Headbutt the dashboard and tell me
- I should have done you better

- I should never have bought that almanac
- this is all my fault

Now step into the DeLorean.

Catapult me out of you.

You are twenty-nine.
You make a rift in the continuum.
You erase my timeline,
my face from your photo,
with your insulting lack of infidelity,
with your slap-sharp beauty,
and I feel like a twat
in my matching yellow jumpsuit and helmet.

Take me back to that future we'll never have.

Turn the crank of truth till I'm ready to homewreck
the marriage of cause and effect.

Return to an empty car park
in the shoulder of night,
five unmarked minutes tapping the hour

and tell me it's over.
It's ok.
I'm ready now.

Participatory Heart

DIANNE: This is great yeah guys? Next steps are to distill the ideas
            down
to one-liners so they don't
die in testing.

I dislike Dianne because she is beautiful like a shampoo advert.
I like her because she is a badass in the boardroom and probably enjoys
            rough sex.

GREG: Ok, but let's not lose the participatory heart of the creative. I'm
superexcited about giving consumers a stake in the
brand.

I like Greg because he looks Jewish.
I dislike him because he is not Jewish despite appearing to be.

KATJA: Just to chip in, can we all please be cognizant of the client's
            preference
for concepts with a future-facing perspective.

I like Katja because she knows the word cognizant.
I dislike her because she used it in a meeting.

MILES: True, but I don't want you guys to restrict your vision to what
            the client will
and won't buy: the objective here is to astonish them with possibilities.

I dislike Miles because he is a Paul Smith suit disguised in a friendly
            jumper.
I like him because he lived in LA and didn't like it.

Percussion

I can't do this.
I know it's late.
I know everyone's waiting, expecting

the thweck of flinging limbs Fred-Astairing
fat sonatas over snare beats cast in metal,

staccato flesh hits dripping on floor tiles,
concubine hips that splay to a Tae Kwon Do kick,
feet flying all around you.

It's just that
I was lying when I told you I could salsa.
I don't know why I did it.

I guess I thought this time would be different,
that the Bomba bass would shoot shock therapy thunder
to my toe touch.
I just wanted to impress you.
I just like you so much.

But now guillotine beats drop fast and precise,
hope bristles and burns in your Christmas Eve eyes
and I have to admit
it's all been lies.
My thighs can't twist the way you want them to.
I'm English.

And I'm far from double-jointed.
At the end of all this, you'll only wind up disappointed.

Trying to be kind as I trip off the stage,
you'll say it's a brave interpretation of the rhythm.

When I elbow you in the neck, you'll tell me
pleasure can't exist without pain.

You'll grow increasingly aware of the way
my knees disagree with each other
as habitually as an old married couple.

You'll hold me closer to block out the guilt
as you look longingly over my shoulder
at *Strictly*.

You'll decorate dance floors with furtive glances that ask,
Are we the worst couple in the room, again?
and by then you'll know
I can't be the reason you smile.
I can't catch you and spin you round.
I'll only get caught up in loose carpet
and knock picture frames to the ground.

As night falls down, you'll lie there feeling like Mother Theresa,
Florence Nightingale, thinking of the big karmic bonus
you're racking up with every step, turn and kiss.

You'll be so miserable, you'll think I must be happy
because fuck knows, one of us has to be.

Eazysleep Podcast Volume 2

Lie down on the bed and close your eyes. Imagine you are lying on soft grass under a clear blue sky. There is no one else around and you are completely safe. Press your palms into the grass, spreading your fingers as wide as you can. Stretch them out   and then relax. As you relax, let your arms and your hands sink deeper into the grass. Now do the same with your legs. And now the back of your head. Your entire body is beginning to feel very heavy. And your mind is at rest. You begin to feel yourself falling into a deep, deep sleep. You are falling asleep. You are falling asleep. Why aren't you falling asleep? You're nearly at the end of this recording. If you don't fall asleep soon, you'll get less than six hours. And you've got that eight-thirty with Stuart from purchasing. Don't forget, you need to iron your stripy shirt. You are feeling sleepy. Start feeling sleepy. You are not thinking about your meeting with Stuart. You are not thinking about what Hannah said at dinner or how she can lie stone-dead asleep next to you, unfazed by the damp, disinterested beat of your lungs or the deafening drum choir of your mind as it keeps you awake for the third time this week. You feel incredibly heavy, as if your body is a sack of bricks sinking into the grass. Imagine that each brick represents a fear or anxiety. Then imagine releasing the bricks one by one. With each brick you become lighter, until you are floating high above them. High above your worries and fears. Imagine if you tried just that little bit harder to make this actually fucking work. You could be asleep right now, getting a decent five-and-a-half hours' rest, ready for your early meeting with twatface Stuart. Imagine you are lying on clear blue grass under a soft sky. Imagine you are lying on a bed of iron filings. Imagine you are lying to yourself and the people you claim to love, every washed-out, homogenous day of your worthless existence. Imagine you'd spent your gap year planting trees in Peru instead of watching Friends repeats with the high-school girlfriend who cheated on you with a young science teacher. You are lying on a bed of increasingly fragile blades of grass, sinking into the rain-sodden grave of your dreams. And why is Stuart calling the shots anyway? You could be his boss by now, if you hadn't had one too many at the summer party and told Mr Webster about your sexual problem. You are lying on a hotbed of scalding regret, while pin-sharp blades of iniquity dig into your kidneys. You sink into the regret, and the transience of the universe taunts you with the kind of godless, unblinking free will that makes you want to pack it all in and go and live on an island. You could make boats. Or open a bar, where you'd play live music with a rugged band of rapscallion locals. You are lying on a boat, on a sea of unblinking free will, drifting further and further away from the pin-sharp iniquities of the people you love. Your limbs are clear blue sky and your head is soft grass. You are beginning to feel sleepy. You are falling asleep. You are nearly asleep. Sleep.

You're a Good Person Sometimes

You are running because running makes you good
and because sometimes running feels good.

You are running because you are a hairy, muscle-wrapped animal
built to move and bellow and beat your chest.

You are running to feel your mass smash against the empty air,
leave stegosaur footprints,

take lane and hill and row and wood for your own
without piss or palms in cement.

You are running from the safety of stillness,
the betrayals of your own body,

the person you love who knows so well what you'll say next,
they no longer hear it.

You speed unstumbling over paving cracks,
use pain to cut your mettle so sleek, it could be someone else's.

You Can Be Your Own Mother

Stella was born at twenty-seven.
No burning wet mess of sperm fucking egg
met her conception. Instead

it started with a child's first sweep of mascara,
tiny feet cuddled into mum's stiletto pumps

and after twenty years of gestation, out she came:
vertigo legs, T-bone hair and all.

Stella was applied, layer by mothwing-fine layer.
She, made of sugar paper, of stardust, of kohl,
all meticulously sewn into place.

Cartilage hand-crafted, nipples appliqué,
the stitching flawless.

She rose out of a shell when she came.
Empire State heart and Restoration waist
out in one big push.

Some people forget their own mind, name,
but not Stella. She'd always known.

Even before kisses. Even at family Christmases
when they still called her Andrew, the seed of her
lay under tongue, waiting to come through.

The Ends of the Earth
for Amma

There has never been anything but this.
Winds blow seeds into bloom and in your mind
turn wheels and shapes I'll never understand,
your sari tucked up to your waist. On the red fabric:
mud stains from 40 years in the fields
with him, planting potatoes with sticks and string, your feet covered in
the scars of a life lived hard, raising heat-lazy babies.
You have earned your place at the head of this house with
the husband you were given to. Married at nine,
pregnant at fifteen: your belly stupa-solid - what else would you expect of
a woman who walked 14 miles to the hospital in labour?
Gathering strength like the hems of skirts. You are a continent.
You speak a language all your own.
The sounds from your mouth bang drums through generations.
I can still hear you with one foot in the soil as
you kick sticks, and the world turns.

You kick sticks, and the world turns.
I can still hear you with one foot in the soil as
the sounds from your mouth bang drums through generations.
You speak a language all your own,
gathering strength like the hems of skirts, you are a continent,
a woman who walked 14 miles to the hospital in labour.
Pregnant at fifteen - your belly stupa-solid - what else would you expect of
the husband you were given to? Married at nine,
you have earned your place at the head of this house with
the scars of a life lived hard, raising heat-lazy babies
with him, planting potatoes with sticks and string, your feet covered in
mud stains from 40 years in the fields,
your sari tucked up to your waist, on the red fabric
turn wheels and shapes I'll never understand.
Winds blow seeds into bloom and in your mind
there has never been anything but this.

Nothing Like the Whites of Your Eyes

I'm not thinking about you
as palm trees weave their tails
through the breeze
    like your hair.

Strong as braids, they sway.
Generations old, they filter the Asian sun
like lemon through a juicer
    and you are so far away.

In the misty mornings on a trek
with Jek from the Czech republic,
mist rises like a mistress's eyebrows
    —not your breath on a cold day

and though it's a few treacle-slow days
since last we kissed
my mainframe remains faithlessly fixed
on this tropical backdrop
on which I've rocked up.

When I look at the moon
in a black sky above a black sea,
the white surface of our planet's satellite
is nothing like the whites of your eyes
and the tittering stars are no less bright
because you are not here with me.

I'm not thinking of a room in Clapham.
I'm drinking mango shakes
indifferent to the changing of your sheets.
I'm eating chili blotted with cheap whisky buckets.
I know nothing of Northern line delays

or mulled wine on rainy Saturdays
                     that turn your dress see-through.

I'm not thinking of you
as I climb breast-shaped mountains.
I am completely centred in the moment
as the scent of pine needles and tea leaves fill my lungs
leaving me so alive that I feel like
                     grabbing you by the hair
                     pulling you down into the earth
                     burying myself in your soil
                     pillaging your land
                     pulling up roots and flowers and daisies.

Fork

Humming for your touch.
       A tuning fork hum
rum-peppered and sun-dumb,
       sloshed with lazy want.

Hum of mosquito,
       of sandfly, scooter,
       of generator
snapping up for morning,
of speedboat engine
       lording lionesque
around the jetty.

A tickle that won't
       lie down, a cockroach
waiting behind the
wash bucket, histamines
       pimpling up where nails
       scratch, where nails pimp up
those hot hot tingles

       that break at night, your
hand over my mouth so
       the honeymoon suite
hear only sea fire.

Poem in Which Aliens Invade My Bedroom

with ray guns gaping
                    at my chest,
with a membraneless shape
                    floating dark on dark
and you'd say,
        drink a glass of water,
go back to bed.

And if that sound is not rat scuffle
                        or upstairs flats
but the tearing of worlds
                choking greys from motherships,

my distress signal
                runs off-script
because you are the one
                in the patchy home videos,

hungry anecdotes,
                the black-splattered myth
that once held me,
                lighter than rain.

The Acre

Much bigger than anyone's. Room and rooms for permutating numbers of slumberers. Our house sucked in playground clingons and thumbsuckers, crossroad crash victims, parties started as mum's car stuttered off to a boyfriend in Shropshire, Chichester, wherever. It was never quiet till university stole sisters. Who returned with strange men. Still everything between the front gate and the back fence smacks of the way back when we jumped off bunk beds. Ran from bumblebees. Spelt ourselves on cassette tape. Interrogated a piece of cheese. We were detectives, diamond hunters, cartoon pigs, lost at sea but between those walls I betrayed everything. Gave myself over when no one was looking, dissolved into noise, hid boys in the secret passageway, skulked in the kitchen on sixth-form lunch break, fed them cereal, Cup-a-soup, chocolate fudge cake, drank Lambrusco unironically, inhaled shallow in alleyways hot through hot tips on cold cigarettes smoked unconvincingly—those lopsided haikus, the dodgy extra syllable hung on my lips and that bonfire smell as we sniffed up JD, kiwi 20/20, weed and deeper still that first love, first real kiss: sunshine, lollipops, rainbows, the apocalypse.

Lightning Source UK Ltd.
Milton Keynes UK
UKHW041204301120
374347UK00002B/81